UNEQUIPPED

Forgiving Your Parents for
What You Didn't Get

CELESTE L. BLACKMAN

Published by So It Is Written, LLC
Detroit, MI
SoItIsWritten.net

Edited by: So It Is Written – www.SoItIsWritten.net

Formatting: Ya Ya Ya Creative – YaYaYaCreative@gmail.com

ISBN: 979-8-9888204-7-5

LCCN: 2024905875

PRINTED AND BOUND IN THE UNITED STATES OF AMERICA

Dedication

⚓ ⚓ ⚓ ⚓ ⚓ ⚓ ⚓ ⚓ ⚓ ⚓ ⚓ ⚓

I want to dedicate this devotional to my amazing parents. I thank you both for giving me what you were capable of giving. I thank you both for your brokenness. Your brokenness and desire to be healed was enough for me to embrace your brokenness and my own. Between the three of us, I have healed and forgiven you both for what you didn't know. You gave me a lot of what I needed to survive in a hole of uncertainty. You taught me to seek God and forgiveness, and to live my life unapologetically. I was told that I would never understand the life of others that chose to take a different route in life. We grew up with friends who may have had the same experiences or maybe a little different. Either way, they're both a choice. Thank you for my life and choosing me to be the difference. May you always rest, knowing you did your best and you were truly appreciated by me.

Love,
Trecie

Introduction

⚓ ⚓ ⚓ ⚓ ⚓ ⚓ ⚓ ⚓ ⚓ ⚓ ⚓ ⚓ ⚓

I pray this devotional brings you healing, forgiveness, peace and wholeness. In a world where imperfections are woven into the fabric of our existence, forgiveness emerges as the radiant light that dispels shadows of resentment. Join me in exploring the divine art of forgiveness, not only as a virtue bestowed upon us, but as a powerful force that heals and restores. Let us embark on this devotional path with open hearts, ready to embrace the profound grace of forgiveness that emanates from the source of all mercy.

The Power of Forgiveness

⚓ ⚓ ⚓ ⚓ ⚓ ⚓ ⚓ ⚓ ⚓ ⚓ ⚓ ⚓

Matthew 6:14-15

"If you forgive those who sin against you, your heavenly Father will forgive you. But if you refuse to forgive others, your Father will not forgive your sins."

We all have a backstory. After being brought up in a household with my functional alcoholic mother and drug-addicted father, life had its share of difficult times. My parents argued, often verbally abusing one another. My mother allowed other people to live with us who were also addicted to drugs and alcohol. You could safely say that I know the smell of crack when I smell it. At age eight, I was molested by a "close friend of the family" and then molested by my cousin's cousin on his father's side of the family. Growing up in the hood, fighting for my life, I watched friends fall to the wayside of neighborhood deaths. Many people judged and talked about me because I chose *not* to shack up at the age of nineteen. In spite of everything I experienced, forgiveness became my best friend.

1. What does true forgiveness look like for you, and how does it differ from merely saying, "I forgive you"?

_____

_____

_____

_____

_____

2. How does forgiving others contribute to personal growth and well-being?

_____

_____

_____

_____

_____

3. Is there a difference between forgiving and forgetting, and should forgiveness always involve reconciliation?

_____

_____

_____

_____

_____

Journal Forgiveness

_____

_____

_____

_____

_____

_____

_____

_____

_____

_____

_____

_____

_____

_____

_____

_____

_____

_____

_____

_____

_____

_____

_____

_____

_____

_____

_____

_____

_____

_____

_____

_____

_____

_____

_____

_____

_____

_____

_____

_____

_____

_____

Allowance is Key

⚓ ⚓ ⚓ ⚓ ⚓ ⚓ ⚓ ⚓ ⚓ ⚓ ⚓ ⚓

Colossians 3:13

"Make allowance for each other's faults, and forgive anyone who offends you. Remember, the Lord forgave you, so you must forgive others."

When we walk in *love*, we are choosing to be merciful about the faults of others. None of us are perfect. Choosing to forgive over hatred and holding grudges, I learned that my thoughts had an influence on my forgiveness toward others; that's when my life changed for the better. I wasn't taught this as a child, so this was a lesson for me. After learning to be more positive and merciful to others' faults, I sought to know more about being broken, mishandled, and unprotected. I knew I had to forgive in order to be forgiven. We don't know what we don't know. Once we learn the dynamics and the truth about a thing, we must execute it in a way that is based on *love*. God is *love*! However, this was extremely difficult because I saw my parents as weak and selfish. Again, they didn't know what they didn't know. Therefore, I had to learn to forgive and walk in *love*.

1. What will you do to be more positive in your thought processes?

_____

_____

_____

_____

_____

2. What does walking in *love* look like for you?

_____

_____

_____

_____

_____

3. What are some positive things you can say to someone after they've offended you?

_____

_____

_____

_____

_____

Journal Forgiveness

_____

_____

_____

_____

_____

_____

_____

_____

_____

_____

_____

_____

_____

_____

_____

_____

_____

_____

_____

_____

_____

_____

_____

_____

_____

_____

_____

_____

_____

_____

_____

_____

_____

_____

_____

_____

_____

_____

_____

_____

_____

_____

We Must Give Grace

⚓ ⚓ ⚓ ⚓ ⚓ ⚓ ⚓ ⚓ ⚓ ⚓ ⚓ ⚓

Ephesians 4:32

"Instead, be kind to each other, tenderhearted, forgiving one another, just as God through Christ has forgiven you."

Most often, we don't know to ask for the backstory of others before we engage in relationships with people. We sometimes judge with negative thoughts and assumptions. Instead of asking, "What's wrong?" we should ask, "What happened?" When we ask, "What happened?" out of love, and in a respectful, loving approach, it opens up the conversation. You won't always receive the answer you want. You may not receive an answer at all. It simply depends on where the person is mentally, emotionally and spiritually. This is why the approach is important. When you do engage in the conversation, it's essential to listen without judgment and allow the individual to speak without interrupting. Let them know it's okay to speak about what happened. Remember that our ancestors were taught whatever goes on in the house stays in the house.

1. Think about a time when you needed grace. How did that make you feel?

    _____

    _____

    _____

    _____

    _____

2. What happened? I challenge you to call the person who offended you and tell them you forgive them.

    _____

    _____

    _____

    _____

    _____

3. Who is this person? How did they respond?

    _____

    _____

    _____

    _____

    _____

Journal Forgiveness

_____

_____

_____

_____

_____

_____

_____

_____

_____

_____

_____

_____

_____

_____

_____

_____

_____

_____

_____

_____

_____

_____

_____

_____

_____

_____

_____

_____

_____

_____

_____

_____

_____

_____

_____

_____

_____

_____

_____

_____

_____

Daddy, I Forgive You

⚓ ⚓ ⚓ ⚓ ⚓ ⚓ ⚓ ⚓ ⚓ ⚓ ⚓ ⚓

Matthew 18:21-22

"Then Peter came to him and asked, 'Lord, how often should I forgive someone who sins against me? Seven times?' 'No, not seven times,' Jesus replied, 'but seventy times seven!'"

At the age of fourteen, my father was stabbed in his upper right arm while his dad was being stabbed to death in front of him. He was broken and traumatized. After learning his backstory, I went to him and told him, "Dad, I forgive you for not being the dad I needed you to be." He wasn't equipped to be a mindful father to me. His dad died in his arms. How can I expect him to be who I needed him to be when he didn't have a dad to teach him how to be a dad? The simple answer: I couldn't.

He then cried in my arms, saying, "Baby, that's all I ever wanted you to know. I didn't know how."

1. Ask your parent about their backstory. What did you learn?

_____

_____

_____

_____

_____

2. How did their response impact you?

_____

_____

_____

_____

_____

3. Did their response give you a clear understanding of how they show up in your life? How?

_____

_____

_____

_____

_____

Journal Forgiveness

_____

_____

_____

_____

_____

_____

_____

_____

_____

_____

_____

_____

_____

_____

_____

_____

_____

_____

_____

_____

_____

_____

_____

_____

_____

_____

_____

_____

_____

_____

_____

_____

_____

_____

_____

_____

_____

_____

_____

_____

_____

_____

_____

_____

They Say Karma Is Real

⚓ ⚓ ⚓ ⚓ ⚓ ⚓ ⚓ ⚓ ⚓ ⚓ ⚓ ⚓ ⚓

Luke 6:37

"Do not judge others, and you will not be judged. Do not condemn others, or it will all come back against you. Forgive others, and you will be forgiven."

Once I figured out that what I put in the universe would come back to me, I realized that some of the decisions I had made out of my own understanding caused me to reap what I had sown. I had three ectopic (tubal) pregnancies in ten months. I almost died in the third surgery. All this occurred after having one abortion. Only to end up getting a partial hysterectomy and being told I can't have any more children. That hurt me tremendously because I wanted to have at least three children. Although I'm so thankful for my daughter, I suffered from the guilt of making the decision to have an abortion.

1. Has it been a time in your life that you felt the guilt of a decision you regretfully made? How did it make you feel?

_____

_____

_____

_____

_____

2. What could you have done differently in that situation?

_____

_____

_____

_____

_____

3. How would you react now if you were in that same position?

_____

_____

_____

_____

_____

Journal Forgiveness

_____

_____

_____

_____

_____

_____

_____

_____

_____

_____

_____

_____

_____

_____

_____

_____

_____

_____

_____

_____

_____

Forgiveness Isn't Always Easy

⚓ ⚓ ⚓ ⚓ ⚓ ⚓ ⚓ ⚓ ⚓ ⚓ ⚓ ⚓

Mark 11:25

"But when you are praying, first forgive anyone you are holding a grudge against, so that your Father in heaven will forgive your sins, too."

As I sat in a room next to the female who'd molested me, I watched her as she was crying, suffering from the loss of a loved one. Surprisingly, I felt horrible for her. I sat there questioning myself about why I wanted to embrace her. This was definitely a test from God. As I struggled with my own emotions, I went into the bathroom with tears in my eyes and prayed for her broken heart.

1. First, forgive yourself for what you didn't know. What is it that you didn't know?

    _____

    _____

    _____

    _____

    _____

2. Grace is in you. How will you forgive yourself?

    _____

    _____

    _____

    _____

    _____

3. Call one person and ask them to forgive you. How did they respond?

    _____

    _____

    _____

    _____

    _____

Journal Forgiveness

_____

_____

_____

_____

_____

_____

_____

_____

_____

_____

_____

_____

_____

_____

_____

_____

_____

_____

_____

_____

_____

_____

_____

_____

_____

_____

_____

_____

_____

_____

_____

_____

_____

_____

_____

_____

_____

_____

_____

_____

Surrender

⚓ ⚓ ⚓ ⚓ ⚓ ⚓ ⚓ ⚓ ⚓ ⚓ ⚓ ⚓ ⚓

James 5:16

"Confess your sins to each other and pray for each other so that you may be healed. The earnest prayer of a righteous person has great power and produces wonderful results."

Although my mother chose alcohol to cope with her brokenness, she was a praying woman. I truly admire her strength. I remember the day I took her to her doctor's appointment. That day, the doctor told her to stop drinking and smoking. Her kidneys were failing. The doctor said if she didn't stop, she would die.

As we drove to her house, she told me, "From this day forward, I will never drink or smoke again. By the end of this year, I will read the complete Bible and boost my prayers." My mother told me she was going to stop drinking and smoking because her children needed her. She surrendered her will for God's will.

1. What does surrendering mean to you?

    _____

    _____

    _____

    _____

    _____

2. In practical terms, what are some strategies or
    practices you do to surrender?

    _____

    _____

    _____

    _____

    _____

3. How does the concept of surrendering make you feel?

    _____

    _____

    _____

    _____

    _____

Journal Forgiveness

_____

_____

_____

_____

_____

_____

_____

_____

_____

_____

_____

_____

_____

_____

_____

_____

_____

_____

_____

_____

Lord, I Need You

Psalm 86:5

"O Lord, you are so good, so ready to forgive, so full of unfailing love for all who ask for your help."

"Lord, I need you," was the beginning of my prayer when I knew I had to forgive my father for emotionally abusing me. I often paid his rent/bills, paid off drug debts, furnished his apartments, washed his body when he couldn't due to him going completely blind, washed his clothes, and bought him food. I took care of my dad, and I was a daddy's girl. All while suffering in silence from him not paying me back and disrespecting me by cursing me out for simply asking him to repay me. It was to the point one day, I literally wanted to fight him because I was so hurt. All my life, I took care of my dad. The first time I was able to rest and not worry about him was when God called him home.

1. In what way did your parents hurt you with their addictions?

   _____

   _____

   _____

   _____

   _____

2. How have you reacted to them from the pain they've caused you?

   _____

   _____

   _____

   _____

   _____

3. Are your parents deceased? If so, in what ways can you make the choice to forgive them and free yourself?

   _____

   _____

   _____

   _____

   _____

4. How were your parents treated as children?

_____

_____

_____

_____

_____

Journal Forgiveness

_____

_____

_____

_____

_____

_____

_____

_____

_____

_____

_____

_____

_____

_____

_____

_____

_____

_____

_____

_____

_____

_____

_____

_____

_____

_____

_____

_____

_____

_____

_____

_____

_____

_____

_____

_____

_____

_____

_____

_____

_____

Have the Conversation and Make Peace

⚓ ⚓ ⚓ ⚓ ⚓ ⚓ ⚓ ⚓ ⚓ ⚓ ⚓ ⚓ ⚓

Isaiah 1:18

"Come now, let's settle this," says the Lord. "Though your sins are like scarlet, I will make them as white as snow. Though they are red like crimson, I will make them as white as wool."

Drug abuse involves the misuse or overuse of legal or illegal substances, leading to negative physical, psychological or social consequences. It can include the use of prescription medications and recreational drugs. Alcohol abuse involves drinking in a way that leads to negative consequences, impacting one's health, relationships, work or overall well-being. I went to my mother and asked her how she felt about us having a conversation about the negative effects of her drinking. She replied, "We can talk about anything." Over a dinner of chicken wings and shrimp fried rice, we had a conversation. With tears in her eyes, she asked me to forgive her, and I accepted.

1. Ask your parents about their backstory. If they are deceased, ask someone who knew them. Ask about their childhood. What did you learn?

   _____

   _____

   _____

   _____

   _____

2. Did their story give you a heartfelt understanding, and how?

   _____

   _____

   _____

   _____

   _____

3. What were the end results of the conversation?

   _____

   _____

   _____

   _____

   _____

4. What things do you want to be delivered from and why?

_____

_____

_____

_____

_____

Journal Forgiveness

_____

_____

_____

_____

_____

_____

_____

_____

_____

_____

_____

_____

_____

_____

_____

_____

_____

_____

_____

_____

_____

_____

_____

_____

_____

_____

_____

_____

_____

_____

_____

_____

_____

_____

_____

_____

_____

_____

_____

_____

_____

_____

Forgive Me for What I Didn't Know

⚓ ⚓ ⚓ ⚓ ⚓ ⚓ ⚓ ⚓ ⚓ ⚓ ⚓ ⚓ ⚓

Acts 3:19

"Now repent of your sins and turn to God,
so that your sins may be wiped away."

Repentance is a profound and sincere change of heart and mind, accompanied by remorse for past wrongs or sins. It involves acknowledging one's mistakes, expressing genuine regret, and actively seeking to make amends for the harm caused. True repentance goes beyond mere verbal expressions of remorse; it involves a commitment to behavioral change and learning from past errors.

The process of repentance can be transformative, leading you to cultivate virtues, develop empathy, and strive for a more positive and ethical way of life. It's so important to repent after you know better so you can live a happy, whole lifestyle.

1. What are your thoughts on repentance?

_____

_____

_____

_____

_____

2. Do you plan to repent? How often will you?

_____

_____

_____

_____

_____

3. Are you willing to change your behavior? How?

_____

_____

_____

_____

_____

Journal Forgiveness

_____

_____

_____

_____

_____

_____

_____

_____

_____

_____

_____

_____

_____

_____

_____

_____

_____

_____

_____

_____

Be Healed

⚓ ⚓ ⚓ ⚓ ⚓ ⚓ ⚓ ⚓ ⚓ ⚓ ⚓ ⚓ ⚓

Psalm 103:12

*"He has removed our sins as far from us
as the east is from the west."*

If God repeatedly removed our sins, why wouldn't we forgive? We shouldn't sin just because He forgives us. But instead, we strive to be the best version of ourselves. Although we are not perfect, we heal and forgive. Walking in love becomes meaningful. The way we think, the things we touch, the things we listen to, the places we go, the people we surround ourselves with, and the things we watch become clearer. Our senses will kick in with a vengeance as we desire to please God and not our own desires.

1. What sins have you been delivered from?

_____

_____

_____

_____

_____

2. How have you been since you decided to be delivered?

_____

_____

_____

_____

_____

3. How are you maintaining?

_____

_____

_____

_____

_____

Journal Forgiveness

_____

_____

_____

_____

_____

_____

_____

_____

_____

_____

_____

_____

_____

_____

_____

_____

_____

_____

_____

_____

_____

The Cleansing

⚓ ⚓ ⚓ ⚓ ⚓ ⚓ ⚓ ⚓ ⚓ ⚓ ⚓ ⚓

1 John 1:9

"But if we confess our sins to him, he is faithful and just to forgive us our sins and to cleanse us from all wickedness."

Confessing our sins can be done in many ways. You could pray, confess to God, and ask Him to cleanse you. You can even journal your confessions to God. You could also confess your faults/issues with someone you trust. Lastly, you can go to the altar with all things. *Come boldly unto the throne of grace, that we may obtain mercy, and find grace to help in time of need* (Hebrews 4:16).

1. Make a list of the ways you choose to confess. Why
    do you choose these ways?

    _____

    _____

    _____

    _____

    _____

2. How will you maintain your cleansing?

    _____

    _____

    _____

    _____

    _____

3. How will you keep yourself from sinning again?

    _____

    _____

    _____

    _____

    _____

Journal Forgiveness

_____

_____

_____

_____

_____

_____

_____

_____

_____

_____

_____

_____

_____

_____

_____

_____

_____

_____

_____

_____

_____

_____

It's A Choice

Proverbs 28:13

"People who conceal their sins will not prosper, but if they confess and turn from them, they will receive mercy."

Someone once told me that we lived different lives, as if I wouldn't be able to understand their story. To a certain degree, I totally understood. But because we grew up in the same neighborhood seeing the same things, our life experiences as children were similar in some ways. It was difficult for me to completely understand because, although we now live differently, we both had a choice. I chose one way, and they chose another way. Our lives are what we make them. It's important to know that we get to decide what path we go on and which direction to walk in.

1. Have you made the choice to forgive? How?

_____

_____

_____

_____

_____

2. When did you make the choice and why?

_____

_____

_____

_____

_____

3. When did you realize you had a choice to forgive, and what caused you to know?

_____

_____

_____

_____

_____

Journal Forgiveness

_____

_____

_____

_____

_____

_____

_____

_____

_____

_____

_____

_____

_____

_____

_____

_____

_____

_____

_____

_____

_____

_____

_____

_____

_____

_____

_____

_____

_____

_____

_____

_____

_____

_____

_____

_____

_____

Unfailing Love

⚓ ⚓ ⚓ ⚓ ⚓ ⚓ ⚓ ⚓ ⚓ ⚓ ⚓ ⚓ ⚓

Micah 7:18

"Where is another God like you, who pardons the guilt of the remnant, overlooking the sins of his special people? You will not stay angry with your people forever, because you delight in showing unfailing love."

Unfailing love is a steadfast and unwavering commitment that endures through challenges and difficulties, remaining constant and resilient. It is a love that transcends circumstances, demonstrating loyalty and devotion, even in the face of adversity.

Unfailing love is characterized by an enduring sense of support, understanding and acceptance, fostering a deep and unbreakable connection between individuals.

This type of love is not contingent upon perfection, but embraces imperfections, recognizing the humanity of the beloved. Unfailing love is often considered a rare and precious quality, symbolizing a bond that withstands the tests of time and fortifies relationships with enduring strength and compassion.

1. Describe an unfailing love.

    _____

    _____

    _____

    _____

    _____

2. What makes this an unfailing love?

    _____

    _____

    _____

    _____

    _____

3. Do you give unfailing love? If so, how?

    _____

    _____

    _____

    _____

    _____

Journal Forgiveness

_____

_____

_____

_____

_____

_____

_____

_____

_____

_____

_____

_____

_____

_____

_____

_____

_____

_____

_____

_____

_____

_____

_____

_____

_____

_____

_____

_____

_____

_____

_____

_____

_____

_____

_____

_____

_____

_____

_____

_____

_____

_____

_____

The Goodness of the Heart

⚓ ⚓ ⚓ ⚓ ⚓ ⚓ ⚓ ⚓ ⚓ ⚓ ⚓ ⚓ ⚓

Romans 12:20-21

"Instead, 'If your enemies are hungry, feed them. If they are thirsty, give them something to drink. In doing this, you will heap burning coals of shame on their heads.' Don't let evil conquer you, but conquer evil by doing good."

I received a "Doing Good In The Hood Award." This really blessed me because, for most of my life, I yearned for the love and support from people to whom I gave it. I didn't know I walked around with this expectation until a friend of mine brought this to my attention. We must be open to receive what we need from the people who don't mind giving to us. I decided to give my heart in places that would give it back. It brought greatness to me to give back to the neighborhood I grew up in, and to see the faces of the people meant everything.

1. What are some practical ways to obtain a good heart?

_____

_____

_____

_____

_____

2. In the face of challenges or conflicts, how can you
    ensure that you will respond with a good heart?

_____

_____

_____

_____

_____

3. To be specific, how does having a good heart
    contribute to personal well-being and mental health?

_____

_____

_____

_____

_____

Journal Forgiveness

_____

_____

_____

_____

_____

_____

_____

_____

_____

_____

_____

_____

_____

_____

_____

_____

_____

_____

_____

_____

_____

_____

_____

_____

_____

_____

_____

_____

_____

_____

_____

_____

_____

_____

_____

_____

_____

_____

_____

_____

_____

_____

Having the Ear to Hear From the Lord

⚓ ⚓ ⚓ ⚓ ⚓ ⚓ ⚓ ⚓ ⚓ ⚓ ⚓ ⚓

Psalm 32:1-2

"Oh, what joy for those whose disobedience is forgiven,
whose sin is put out of sight! Yes, what joy for those whose
record the Lord has cleared of guilt,
whose lives are lived in complete honesty!"

Many people say, "Something told me to go right, but I went left," meaning our first mind tells us to do something beneficial, but we don't always listen. I believe that the "first mind" is the discerning voice of the Lord. I didn't always listen because, just like others, I wasn't always obedient to His voice. His voice will direct us; we just need to listen the first time. Listening to His voice can be life-changing.

1. Do you believe you have the ear to hear from the Lord? Why?

_____

_____

_____

_____

_____

2. How can you become more connected to His voice?

_____

_____

_____

_____

_____

3. Who will you seek to become stronger in this area of your life?

_____

_____

_____

_____

_____

Journal Forgiveness

_____

_____

_____

_____

_____

_____

_____

_____

_____

_____

_____

_____

_____

_____

_____

_____

_____

_____

_____

_____

He's a Forgiving God

⚓ ⚓ ⚓ ⚓ ⚓ ⚓ ⚓ ⚓ ⚓ ⚓ ⚓ ⚓ ⚓

1 John 2:1-2

*"My dear children, I am writing this to you so that you
will not sin. But if anyone does sin, we have an advocate
who pleads our case before the Father. He is Jesus Christ,
the one who is truly righteous. He himself is the sacrifice
that atones for our sins—and not only our sins
but the sins of all the world."*

It is written that God is a forgiving God. As you move into your journey of forgiveness of others, let's not forget to forgive ourselves. Often, we hold on to things we can't control or the things we regret. This does nothing more than keep you in bondage. You must forgive yourself for all things. I was in a silent depression after having an abortion because I felt as if I had committed the biggest sin ever. It was difficult to forgive myself.

1. Have you forgiven yourself? How?

    _____

    _____

    _____

    _____

    _____

2. Do you believe God is a forgiving God? Why?

    _____

    _____

    _____

    _____

    _____

3. How will you forgive yourself moving forward?

    _____

    _____

    _____

    _____

    _____

Journal Forgiveness

_____

_____

_____

_____

_____

_____

_____

_____

_____

_____

_____

_____

_____

_____

_____

_____

_____

_____

_____

_____

_____

_____

_____

_____

_____

_____

_____

_____

_____

_____

_____

_____

_____

_____

_____

_____

_____

_____

_____

_____

_____

_____

_____

Even When It Hurts

⚓ ⚓ ⚓ ⚓ ⚓ ⚓ ⚓ ⚓ ⚓ ⚓ ⚓ ⚓ ⚓

Luke 17:3-4

"So watch yourselves! If another believer sins, rebuke that person; then if there is repentance, forgive. Even if that person wrongs you seven times a day and each time turns again and asks forgiveness, you must forgive."

Over the years, I've had to forgive so many people who hurt me. Was it easy? No! Did I have moments when I wanted to react in an ungodly way? Absolutely! What would that have done for me besides being held accountable by God? If I wanted God to forgive me, I had to forgive even when it hurt, and I didn't want to. I prayed that hurt off my heart and continued asking for forgiveness for myself and for others.

1. What is hurting you?

_____

_____

_____

_____

_____

2. Why are you holding on to it?

_____

_____

_____

_____

_____

3. When will you let it go?

_____

_____

_____

_____

_____

Journal Forgiveness

_____

_____

_____

_____

_____

_____

_____

_____

_____

_____

_____

_____

_____

_____

_____

_____

_____

_____

_____

_____

_____

_____

_____

_____

_____

_____

_____

_____

_____

_____

_____

_____

_____

_____

_____

_____

_____

_____

_____

_____

_____

_____

_____

_____

_____

_____

_____

_____

_____

_____

_____

_____

_____

_____

_____

_____

_____

_____

_____

_____

_____

_____

_____

_____

_____

Forgiveness is For You

⚓ ⚓ ⚓ ⚓ ⚓ ⚓ ⚓ ⚓ ⚓ ⚓ ⚓ ⚓

Jeremiah 31:34

"And they will not need to teach their neighbors, nor will they need to teach their relatives, saying, 'You should know the Lord.' For everyone, from the least to the greatest, will know me already," says the Lord. "And I will forgive their wickedness, and I will never again remember their sins."

So often, we have expectations for others that we didn't require of them at the beginning of the relationship. Before we were born, our parents named us. Them being mom and dad, the expectations were that they had it all together. It's said, "Why would they have children if they wanted to abuse or neglect them?" I don't believe it's what they wanted to do. But more importantly, it's what they didn't know *how* to do.

1. How would you feel if your parents rejected answering your questions about their backstory?

_____

_____

_____

_____

_____

2. How will you react if you don't get the answers you are looking for?

_____

_____

_____

_____

_____

3. Will you forgive in spite of their response?

_____

_____

_____

_____

_____

Journal Forgiveness

Guilt is Not of God

⚓ ⚓ ⚓ ⚓ ⚓ ⚓ ⚓ ⚓ ⚓ ⚓ ⚓ ⚓

Psalm 51:1-2

"Have mercy on me, O God, because of your unfailing love. Because of your great compassion, blot out the stain of my sins. Wash me clean from my guilt. Purify me from my sin."

I have prayed this Scripture over my life many times. Because I understood my sins, I knew the love of God when I prayed for myself through my last surgery. My doctor said that in all his forty years of practicing medicine, he's never cried before surgery. He said he didn't know if the Lord was going to take my life on that table.

But, if so, I prayed and pleaded with God. In that prayer, I said, "God, I promise not to feel guilty again."

1. Are you holding on to guilt? What is it?

_____

_____

_____

_____

_____

2. Who do you blame? Why?

_____

_____

_____

_____

_____

3. How much longer will you hold on to the guilt? Will you choose to be free?

_____

_____

_____

_____

_____

Journal Forgiveness

When You've Let Your Unforgiveness Turn Into Your Disease

⚓ ⚓ ⚓ ⚓ ⚓ ⚓ ⚓ ⚓ ⚓ ⚓ ⚓ ⚓ ⚓

Psalm 103:3

"He forgives all my sins and heals all my diseases."

*P*sychosocial factors like mental health, stress and emotional well-being can impact your physical health. Chronic stress, for example, has been linked to the development or exacerbation of conditions such as cardiovascular disease and digestive disorders. It is vital to our health that we free ourselves from all hurt and hatred. If we want to live happily and wholly, we must do as God wants us to do: love, forgive and give unto others as He leads us.

1. Will you choose forgiveness or disease? Why?

    _____

    _____

    _____

    _____

    _____

2. What sticks out to you most in this list of psychosocial factors and why?

    _____

    _____

    _____

    _____

    _____

3. Give an example of something you've physically experienced from holding unforgiveness. What did it teach you?

    _____

    _____

    _____

    _____

    _____

Journal Forgiveness

_____

_____

_____

_____

_____

_____

_____

_____

_____

_____

_____

_____

_____

_____

_____

_____

_____

_____

_____

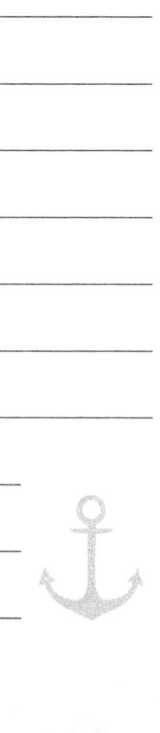

Free of Condemnation

⚓ ⚓ ⚓ ⚓ ⚓ ⚓ ⚓ ⚓ ⚓ ⚓ ⚓ ⚓

Romans 8:1-2

*"So now there is no condemnation for those who belong to
Christ Jesus. And because you belong to him,
the power of the life-giving Spirit has freed you
from the power of sin that leads to death."*

Imagine living your life with no condemnation. Wouldn't that be ecstatic? You could have a life-giving spirit all the time, through every situation, in abundance for every decision you make. God will be pleased with your heart because you made the choice.

1. What would a life free from condemnation look like to you?

   _____

   _____

   _____

   _____

   _____

2. How would your perspective shift when you're living a life such as this?

   _____

   _____

   _____

   _____

   _____

3. Will you encourage others to seek the same? Why?

   _____

   _____

   _____

   _____

   _____

Journal Forgiveness

_____

_____

_____

_____

_____

_____

_____

_____

_____

_____

_____

_____

_____

_____

_____

_____

_____

_____

_____

_____

_____

_____

The Newness of God's Love

⚓ ⚓ ⚓ ⚓ ⚓ ⚓ ⚓ ⚓ ⚓ ⚓ ⚓ ⚓

2 Corinthians 5:17

*"This means that anyone who belongs to Christ has become
a new person. The old life is gone; a new life has begun!"*

My walk was different. My talk became different. I had a reason to wake up and go about my day. This gave me the strength to feed God's children who were less fortunate and clothe the ones who bared their backs against the walls of life.

1. How do you think this blessing would look for you?

_____

_____

_____

_____

_____

2. Do you believe you deserve this life and why?

_____

_____

_____

_____

_____

3. Who else do you believe deserves this life besides you?

_____

_____

_____

_____

_____

Journal Forgiveness

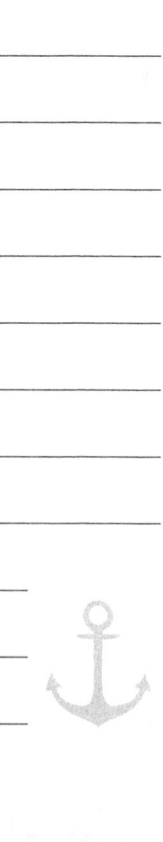

Just When I Thought I Couldn't Do It

⚓ ⚓ ⚓ ⚓ ⚓ ⚓ ⚓ ⚓ ⚓ ⚓ ⚓ ⚓

Psalm 130:3-4

"Lord, if you kept a record of our sins, who,
O Lord, could ever survive? But you offer forgiveness,
that we might learn to fear you."

I pray before approaching any situation. I ask God to intercede in the conversation with openness and love for all parties involved. I've done this in my car, in the bathroom in a restaurant, even while holding the hands of the person I'm having the conversation with.

1. How will you do this?

    _____

    _____

    _____

    _____

    _____

2. Who are you willing to do this with? Ask yourself,
    "What would God do?"

    _____

    _____

    _____

    _____

    _____

3. Do you feel it's worth doing and why?

    _____

    _____

    _____

    _____

    _____

Journal Forgiveness

_____

_____

_____

_____

_____

_____

_____

_____

_____

_____

_____

_____

_____

_____

_____

_____

_____

_____

_____

_____

_____

The Power of Forgiveness

⚓ ⚓ ⚓ ⚓ ⚓ ⚓ ⚓ ⚓ ⚓ ⚓ ⚓ ⚓ ⚓

Isaiah 43:25

"I—yes, I alone—will blot out your sins for my own sake and will never think of them again."

If God no longer thinks of our sins after He's blotted them out, why should we? Let go and let God! It's time, and you deserve to be free. Free from all that has kept you in bondage. God loves you in spite of your sins. Choose to love others in spite of their sins.

1. Will you blot out the sins of your parents?

    _____

    _____

    _____

    _____

    _____

2. Are you willing to never think of the sins again and why?

    _____

    _____

    _____

    _____

    _____

3. What's your plan to utilize this in your daily living?

    _____

    _____

    _____

    _____

    _____

Journal Forgiveness

_____

_____

_____

_____

_____

_____

_____

_____

_____

_____

_____

_____

_____

_____

_____

_____

_____

_____

_____

_____

_____

_____

_____

_____

_____

_____

_____

_____

_____

_____

_____

_____

_____

_____

_____

_____

_____

_____

_____

_____

_____

_____

_____

_____

_____

Everlasting Love

⚓ ⚓ ⚓ ⚓ ⚓ ⚓ ⚓ ⚓ ⚓ ⚓ ⚓ ⚓

Romans 8:38-39

"And I am convinced that nothing can ever separate us from God's love. Neither death nor life, neither angels nor demons, neither our fears for today nor our worries about tomorrow— not even the powers of hell can separate us from God's love."

The concept of never separating often carries profound significance in relationships, symbolizing an unbreakable bond that withstands challenges and trials. The idea of never separating reflects a steadfast promise to remain united, no matter the circumstances. It signifies a pledge of loyalty and resilience, emphasizing the enduring nature of a connection that refuses to be divided.

The commitment to never separate extends beyond a physical presence, encapsulating emotional and spiritual unity and fostering a sense of security and trust. Whether applied to friendships, partnerships or family bonds, the principle of never separating underscores the strength of enduring connections that persist through time and adversity. These are the words from the Most High, our God.

1. Have you ever experienced everlasting love outside of God?

   _____

   _____

   _____

   _____

   _____

2. Do you believe God's love is everlasting? Why?

   _____

   _____

   _____

   _____

   _____

3. Are you willing to give everlasting love as God will always and forever give it to you?

   _____

   _____

   _____

   _____

   _____

Journal Forgiveness

_____

_____

_____

_____

_____

_____

_____

_____

_____

_____

_____

_____

_____

_____

_____

_____

_____

_____

_____

_____

_____

_____

So Far Away

⚓ ⚓ ⚓ ⚓ ⚓ ⚓ ⚓ ⚓ ⚓ ⚓ ⚓ ⚓

Psalm 103:10-12

"He does not punish us for all our sins; he does not deal harshly with us, as we deserve. For his unfailing love toward those who fear him is as great as the height of the heavens above the earth. He has removed our sins as far from us as the east is from the west."

Being willing to go far beyond your expectations to be healed and whole is something that you'll never regret doing. Remember that all the work you do is for *you*. You are making the choice for you and no one else. Do not move harshly, but always in love.

1. How far are you willing to go to be healed and whole?
   Why?

   _____

   _____

   _____

   _____

   _____

2. Do you believe working diligently to become healed
   and whole is worth doing? Why?

   _____

   _____

   _____

   _____

   _____

3. Daily, how can you better choose you over everyone
   else?

   _____

   _____

   _____

   _____

   _____

Journal Forgiveness

_____

_____

_____

_____

_____

_____

_____

_____

_____

_____

_____

_____

_____

_____

_____

_____

_____

_____

_____

_____

_____

_____

It's Forgotten

Hebrews 8:12

"And I will forgive their wickedness,
and I will never again remember their sins."

Forgive your parents. They've done the best they could with what they had. If they were never in your life, that may be a blessing, as well. God still requires forgiveness. This commandment emphasizes the moral and ethical duty to show reverence, gratitude and love to one's parents. Fostering family relationships and social harmony underscores the importance of family bonds and the role parents play in the upbringing and well-being of their children.

1. Why wouldn't you forgive someone?

_____

_____

_____

_____

_____

2. When would it be okay for God not to forgive you and why?

_____

_____

_____

_____

_____

3. What do your parents need to be forgiven for?

_____

_____

_____

_____

_____

Journal Forgiveness

Walk in Love

⚓ ⚓ ⚓ ⚓ ⚓ ⚓ ⚓ ⚓ ⚓ ⚓ ⚓ ⚓

1 Peter 3:9

*"Don't repay evil for evil. Don't retaliate with insults
when people insult you. Instead, pay them back with a
blessing. That is what God has called you to do,
and he will grant you his blessing."*

Walk in love no matter what. Every ill decision you make, you will have to reap the benefits (or lack thereof) from that decision. God loves a cheerful giver. Giving love and paying them back with a blessing is a true gift to God.

1. Walking in love can be challenging. Do you believe you can do it?

_____

_____

_____

_____

_____

2. What does life look like for you if you don't walk in love?

_____

_____

_____

_____

_____

3. Counting all blessings, will you choose God's way or your own?

_____

_____

_____

_____

_____

Journal Forgiveness

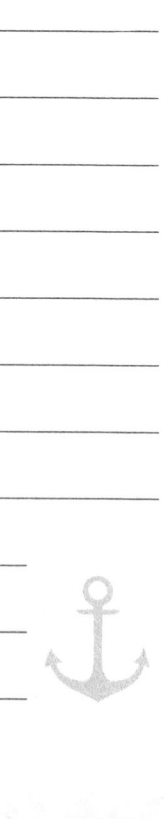

If Only My People

⚓ ⚓ ⚓ ⚓ ⚓ ⚓ ⚓ ⚓ ⚓ ⚓ ⚓ ⚓ ⚓

2 Chronicles 7:14

"Then if my people who are called by my name will humble themselves and pray and seek my face and turn from their wicked ways, I will hear from heaven and will forgive their sins and restore their land."

Humbling oneself involves recognizing and accepting personal imperfections, mistakes, and areas for improvement. It's an honest appraisal of one's own strengths and weaknesses. A humble person tends to be empathetic and compassionate toward others, understanding that everyone has struggles and challenges.

Humility is linked to a willingness to learn from others. It means being open to new ideas, perspectives and experiences, and understanding that growth comes from continuous learning. Demonstrated through respect for others, regardless of their background, status, or beliefs. It involves treating everyone with kindness and dignity.

Humbling oneself also includes taking responsibility for one's actions. When mistakes are made, a humble person acknowledges them, learns from them, and seeks to make amends. Humility contrasts with arrogance or excessive pride. It involves resisting the urge to boast, belittle others, or seek constant validation.

A humble person often expresses gratitude for the support, opportunities and positive aspects of life. This acknowledgment of blessings contributes to a humble and appreciative mindset.

1. Why will you choose to be humble?

_____

_____

_____

_____

_____

2. How will you seek God's face?

_____

_____

_____

_____

_____

3. How will you turn from your wicked ways?

_____

_____

_____

_____

_____

Journal Forgiveness

_____

_____

_____

_____

_____

_____

_____

_____

_____

_____

_____

_____

_____

_____

_____

_____

_____

_____

_____

Free at Last

Psalm 119:165

*"Those who love your instructions have great peace
and do not stumble."*

When I decided to follow the instructions of God, I was set free. My life totally changed. The timing was perfect. Every hurt, disappointment and failure was so worth it. My life experiences weren't all bad. They definitely weren't all good. But I thank God for His grace and mercy. You will be healed.

1. How will you choose to follow God's instructions?

    _____

    _____

    _____

    _____

    _____

2. Why is it important to you to follow His instructions?

    _____

    _____

    _____

    _____

    _____

3. Tell me about a time you stumbled and how you felt afterward.

    _____

    _____

    _____

    _____

    _____

Journal Forgiveness

Sample Forgiveness Letter

⚓ ⚓ ⚓ ⚓ ⚓ ⚓ ⚓ ⚓ ⚓ ⚓ ⚓ ⚓

Date

Dear [*Recipient's Name*],

I hope this letter finds you well. I have been reflecting on our relationship and the events that transpired, and I believe it's time for me to extend my forgiveness.

I forgive you for [*specific incident or situation*].

[*Share your feelings or thoughts about the incident*].

[*Express any hurt or pain you may have felt*].

[*Acknowledge that forgiveness is a process and commitment*].

I recognize that we are all imperfect beings, capable of making mistakes. In extending my forgiveness, I release any resentment or anger I may have been holding onto.

[*Express your desire for healing and moving forward and share any positive intentions or hopes for the future*].

May this forgiveness pave the way for healing and restoration in our relationship. I believe in the power of reconciliation and growth.

Wishing you peace and understanding,

Your Name

About the Author

⚓ ⚓ ⚓ ⚓ ⚓ ⚓ ⚓ ⚓ ⚓ ⚓ ⚓ ⚓

What many would consider to be a state of brokenness Celeste L. Blackman used as building blocks for success. From sexual abuse and the loss of her best friend, then her mother, father and oldest sister, to the loss of other family members to gun violence, Celeste knows firsthand what it's like to be broken—mentally, spiritually and emotionally. Using her personal experience as a weapon of warfare to fight for others, she has made it her life's purpose to assist children and adults alike who have lost their parents or endured life's struggles and feel hopeless. Through a supportive, structured process, she not only positions clients to live a successful, fruitful life—but she teaches them to lead others into a life of fulfillment.

Through her programs, her clients experience authentic healing and wholeness that they once thought they'd never find. As a coach to many, Celeste works diligently to make sure her clients feel safe, encouraged and confident when they leave her presence. Having obtained her educational experience from The CAPP Institute for Coaching and

Positive Psychology, Moody Bible Institute of Michigan, and the Breakthrough Coaching & Leadership Academy, her background has led her to be a highly sought after partner for many organizations. In addition to formerly serving on the advisory board of Adams Butzel Recreation Complex, she's been fortunate to collaborate with Women Creating Caring Communities, Sow a Seed Youth Organization, Women of Virtue and the Amazing Woman Network. She also co-founded her own women's social group, Women of Resilience.

When she's not helping others move their missions forward in and around the local community, she's busy hosting her signature programs, such as: Ladies with Visions, the Healing and Prosperity Goal Setting Program, Healing Beyond Me, and the Kingya Youth Program. Annually, Celeste also organizes a back-to-school rally, Easter Kiddie Disco, a holiday meal program and a women's retreat. Her work as a personal development resilience coach, community advocate and woman of influence also led her to be awarded the Spirit of Detroit Award, as well as the "Doin' Good in the Hood" Award, Passion Award, Certificate of Appreciation Award and Distinguished Service Award. She's also utilized her voice on Wow! That's Crazy! Podcast as co-host and TheWONTVPodcast. In addition to launching her debut solo book project, *Unequipped: Forgiving Your Parents for What You Didn't Get,* in 2024, Celeste is also a co-author in *Marriage Uncut III: Prospering in a Pandemic.*

Today, Celeste moves forward through The Healing and Prosperity nonprofit, the Prosperity Living Preschool, and the Kingya Youth Foundation, supporting children from all walks of life with coaching, counseling, mentorship and guidance. She fills gaps of poverty with pieces of prosperity, eventually positioning people to help others soar beyond their circumstance or environment. In a world of chaos and confusion, she makes it a point to be the calm of someone's storm—balancing the scales of others so they can maintain mental stability at all times, in all seasons. For interviews, speaking engagements or more information on upcoming events, email healingandprosperityfoundation@yahoo.com or follow Healing & Prosperity Foundation on Facebook. You can also visit www.healingandprosperity.org or call 313.523.8540.

Notes